These are Raina the dog's paw prints.

Ruuxa and Raina were three years old when they made these paw prints.

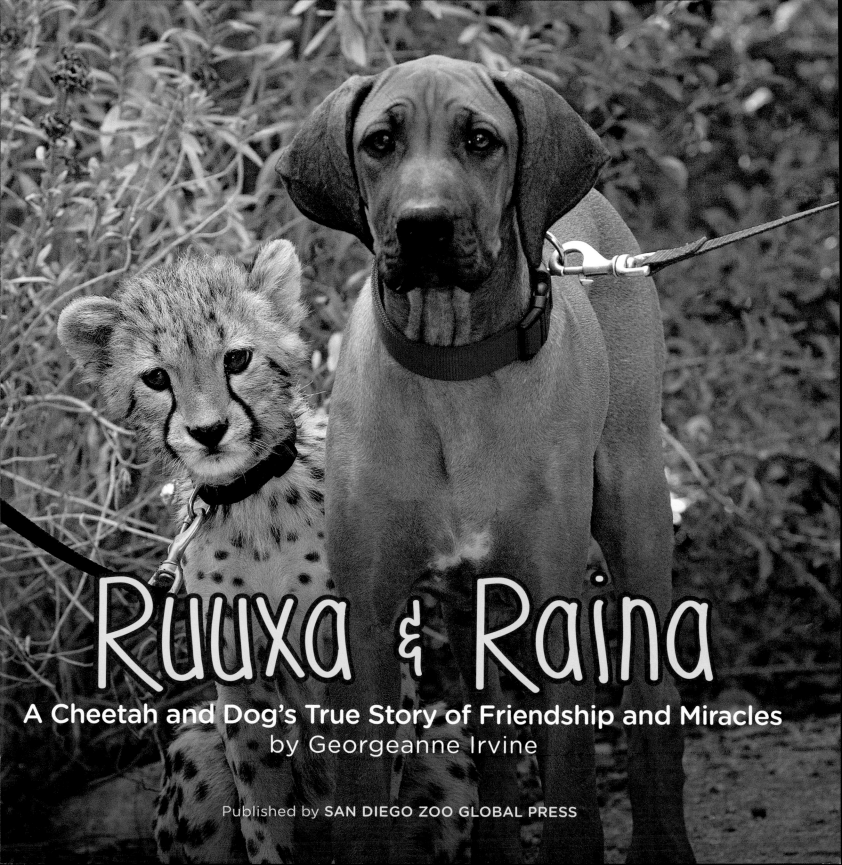

Ruuxa & Raina

A Cheetah and Dog's True Story of Friendship and Miracles
by Georgeanne Irvine

Published by SAN DIEGO ZOO GLOBAL PRESS

Ruuxa & Raina: A Cheetah and Dog's True Story of Friendship and Miracles was published by San Diego Zoo Global Press in association with Blue Sneaker Press. Through these publishing efforts, we seek to inspire multiple generations to care about wildlife, the natural world, and conservation.

San Diego Zoo Global is committed to leading the fight against extinction. It saves species worldwide by uniting its expertise in animal care and conservation science with its dedication to inspire a passion for nature.

Douglas G. Myers, President and Chief Executive Officer
Shawn Dixon, Chief Operating Officer
Yvonne Miles, Corporate Director of Retail
Georgeanne Irvine, Director of Corporate Publishing
San Diego Zoo Global
P.O. Box 120551
San Diego, CA 92112-0551
sandiegozoo.org | 619-231-1515

San Diego Zoo Global's publishing partner is Blue Sneaker Press, an imprint of Southwestern Publishing Group, Inc., 2451 Atrium Way, Nashville, TN 37214. Southwestern Publishing Group is a wholly owned subsidiary of Southwestern Family of Companies, Nashville, Tennessee.

Christopher G. Capen, President, Southwestern Publishing Group
Carrie Hasler, Publisher, Blue Sneaker Press
Kristin Connelly, Managing Editor
Lori Sandstrom, Art Director/Graphic Designer
swpublishinggroup.com | 800-358-0560

ISBN: 978-1-943198-06-1
Library of Congress Control Number: 2018930226
Printed in China
10 9 8 7 6 5 4 3

To Ruuxa, Raina, and Little Rae,
who taught me that miracles really happen!
And to their trainers who never gave up hope.

Acknowledgments:

THANK YOU TO THE FOLLOWING PEOPLE FOR HELPING ME BRING RUUXA AND RAINA'S STORY TO LIFE:

Janet Rose-Hinostroza, Kristyn Sargent, Annette Russell, Shannon Smith, Kim Hanley, Larissa Brecht, Ashley Gordon, Jessica Holland, Callie Jordheim, Kelly Devecchio, Danielle Alifano, Alanna Cappelli, Samantha Passovoy, Susie Ekard, Melodi Tayles, Patty Cassady, Denise Carson, Eileen Neff, Julie Nute, Ken Bohn, Carrie Hasler, Lori Sandstrom, Mary Sekulovich, Lisa Bissi, Jen MacEwen, Kim Turner, Autumn Nelson, Victoria Garrison, Angel Chambosse, Jeff Zuba, DVM, Nadine Lamberski, DVM, Jim Oosterhuis, DVM, Sean Aiken, DVM, Douglas Myers, Shawn Dixon, Yvonne Miles, Diane Cappelletti, Chris Capen, Peggy Blessing, and Judi Myers.

PHOTO CREDITS

Ken Bohn: title page 1, 4, 5, 6, 7 right, 8, 9, 10, 11, 12, 16, 17, 18, 19, 20, 21, 22 upper left, 23 upper right, 25 lower right, 28 lower left, 30 top, 31. **Georgeanne Irvine:** 3, 13, 22 lower right, 23 bottom, 24, 25 upper left, 26, 27, 29, 32, 33, back cover. **Patty Cassady:** front cover, 7 top left. **Jeff Zuba, DVM:** 14, 15 right. **Kristyn Sargent:** 30 lower left. **Tammy Spratt:** 28 upper left. **Julie Nute:** back jacket flap. **Shutterstock:** 34, 35, 36.

Welcome to a New Home!

A precious baby cheetah chirped loudly as the cargo jet he was riding in landed at San Diego International Airport. The two-week-old cub was born at a zoo in Oregon, but his mother was not able to care for him. So now he would be raised by people at his new home, the San Diego Zoo Safari Park.

By the time the cheetah reached the Safari Park's animal care center, the little guy was hungry. The cub snuggled in his keeper's arms as he slurped milk from a bottle. After he finished eating, the keeper gently patted the cub's back to burp him and then laid him on a soft blanket for a nap.

The cub was named Ruuxa (Rōok-suh), which means "spirit" in Somali. Although he was small—he weighed less than three pounds—Ruuxa had lots of energy and wanted to have things his way! He chirped to let the keepers know when he was hungry or when he wanted to play.

Baby cheetahs make a chirping sound, just like a bird!

Two weeks after Ruuxa arrived at the Safari Park, he met a special animal that was going to become his playmate and best friend for life—Raina. But Raina wasn't a cheetah— she was a five-week-old Rhodesian ridgeback puppy!

Raina means "guardian" in German.

Best Buddies

Raina was a sweet puppy, although at eight pounds, she was more than twice Ruuxa's size. When they first met, Ruuxa stomped his feet and chirped at her. Then he got braver—he pounced on Raina's head and ran away!

Soon, they loved wrestling with each other, but the puppy was always gentle with Ruuxa. Raina seemed to know that she was much bigger than her cheetah cub friend.

Since Ruuxa and Raina were raised together as cub and pup, they became like brother and sister.

While they were getting to know each other, Ruuxa and Raina played together every day but slept in different areas. It wasn't long before they became best buddies and wanted to be together all the time.

A Problem with Ruuxa's Legs

When Ruuxa was nine weeks old, the keepers noticed that his legs were bowed. The veterinarians hoped they would grow straight as he got older. Ruuxa needed strong, healthy legs to be able to run fast like other cheetahs.

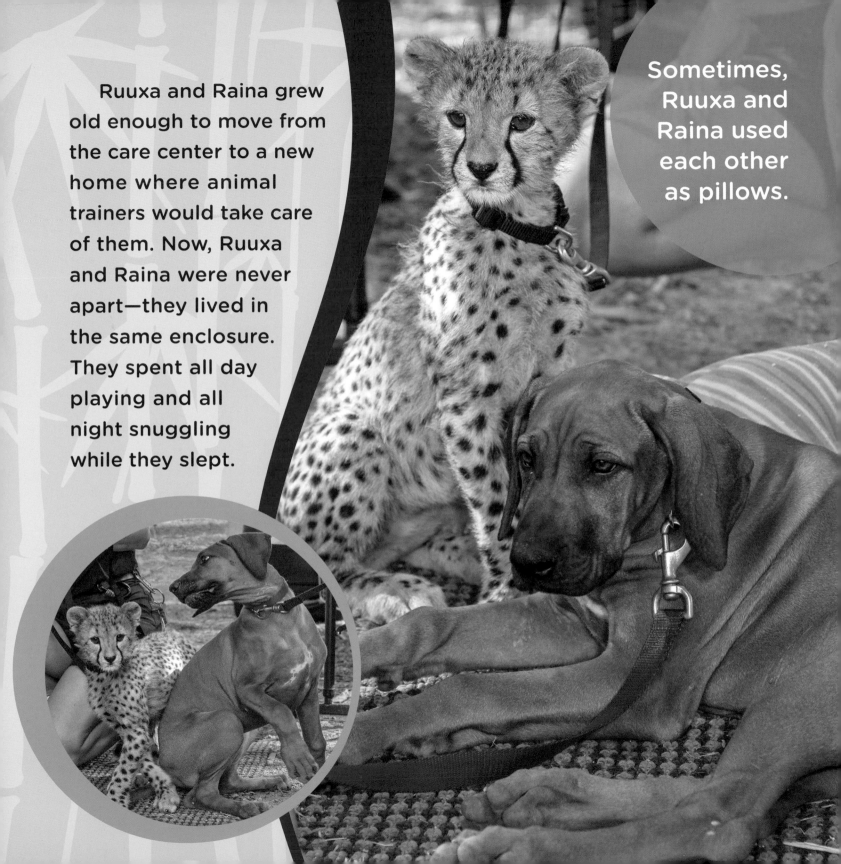

Ruuxa and Raina grew old enough to move from the care center to a new home where animal trainers would take care of them. Now, Ruuxa and Raina were never apart—they lived in the same enclosure. They spent all day playing and all night snuggling while they slept.

Sometimes, Ruuxa and Raina used each other as pillows.

Animal Ambassadors

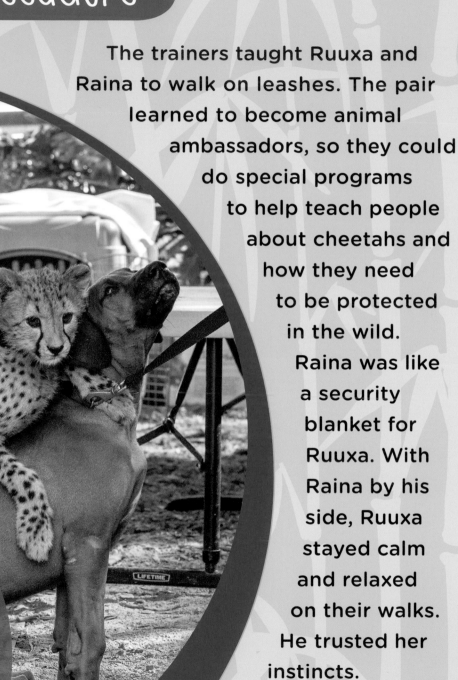

The trainers taught Ruuxa and Raina to walk on leashes. The pair learned to become animal ambassadors, so they could do special programs to help teach people about cheetahs and how they need to be protected in the wild. Raina was like a security blanket for Ruuxa. With Raina by his side, Ruuxa stayed calm and relaxed on their walks. He trusted her instincts.

While Ruuxa was still little, his bowed legs didn't prevent him from playing or walking.

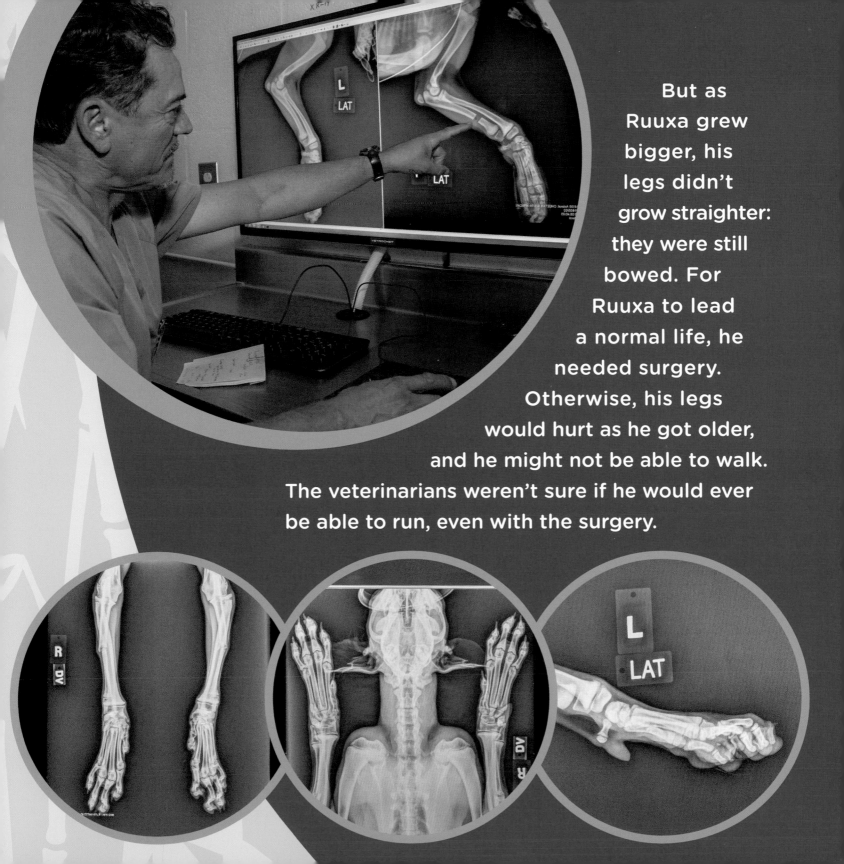

But as Ruuxa grew bigger, his legs didn't grow straighter: they were still bowed. For Ruuxa to lead a normal life, he needed surgery. Otherwise, his legs would hurt as he got older, and he might not be able to walk. The veterinarians weren't sure if he would ever be able to run, even with the surgery.

Surgery Day

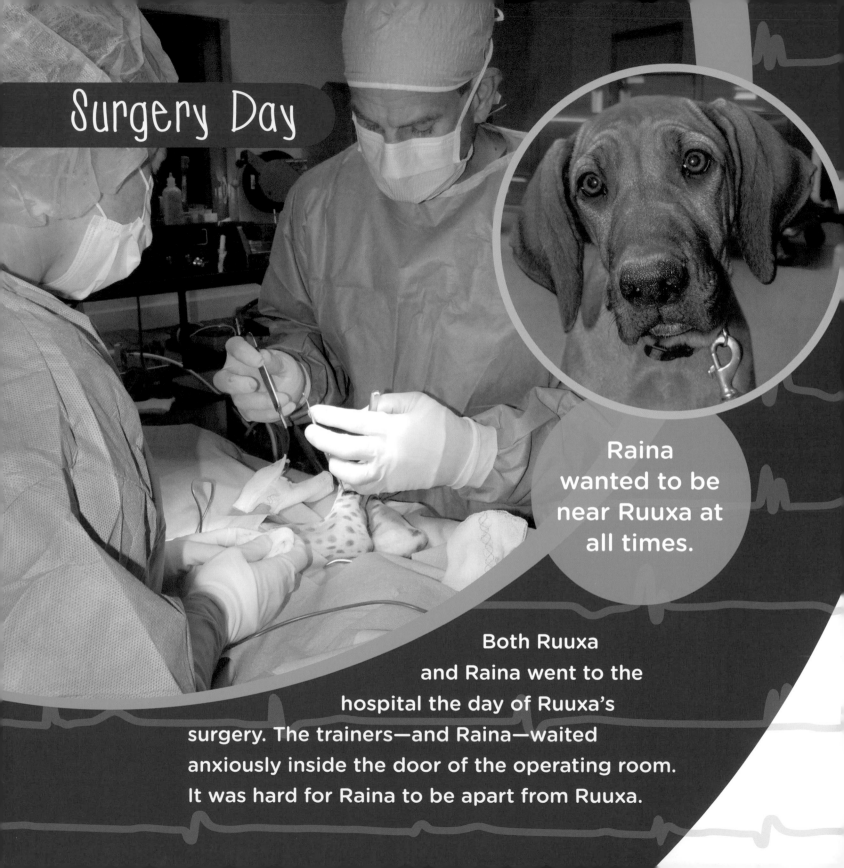

Raina wanted to be near Ruuxa at all times.

Both Ruuxa and Raina went to the hospital the day of Ruuxa's surgery. The trainers—and Raina—waited anxiously inside the door of the operating room. It was hard for Raina to be apart from Ruuxa.

After the operation, Raina sat near Ruuxa as he recovered in a kennel. Ruuxa had been given medicine to make him sleep during the surgery, so he didn't wake up right away. The trainers could tell Raina was concerned. When Ruuxa finally woke up, he whimpered, then chirped, and batted at the door with his paw. As one of the trainers opened the door, Raina squeezed in and snuggled up to her cheetah friend.

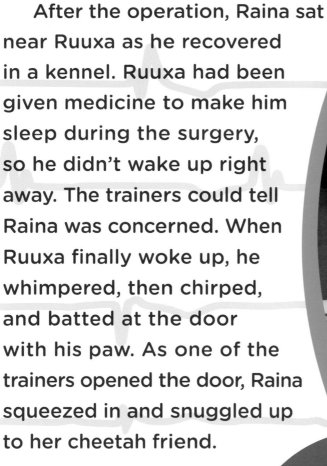

Ruuxa immediately calmed down with Raina by his side again.

No Slowing Down for Ruuxa!

The trainers tried to limit Ruuxa's activity after the surgery so his legs could heal, but he wouldn't slow down. Within a day he chewed his bandages off and was going for walks with Raina. And even though the veterinarians weren't sure Ruuxa would ever be able to run, *he* didn't know that and began to run anyway! Everyone was ecstatic!

Three months
after the surgery,
Ruuxa and Raina
went to play in a big,
grassy enclosure. They
raced through the grass,
around trees, and up and down
hills. They climbed on boulders
and even tackled each other.

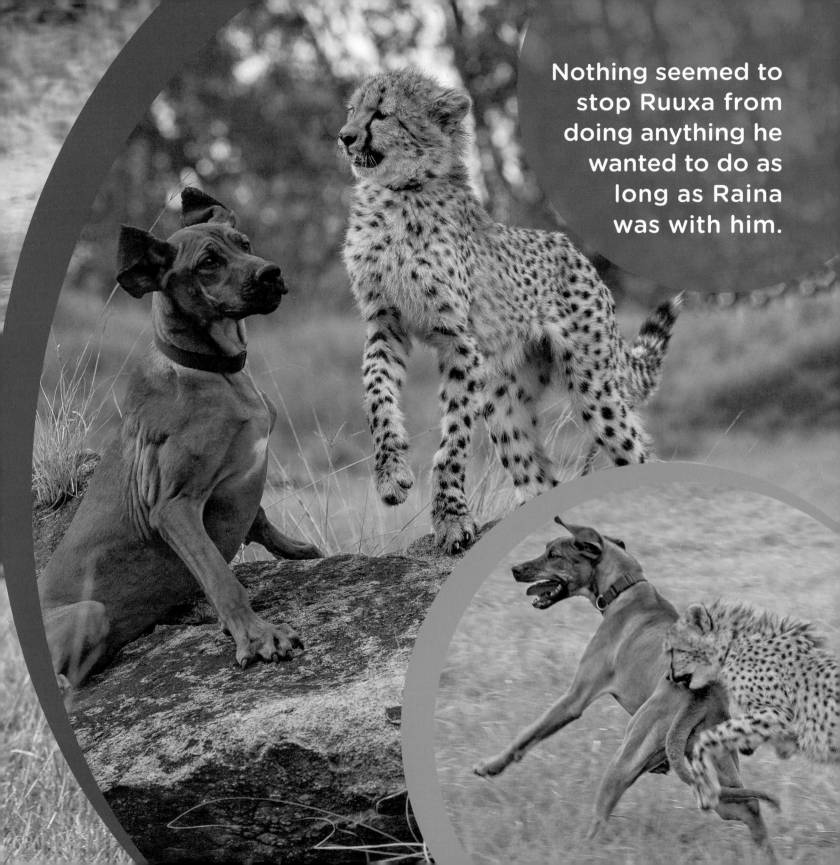

Nothing seemed to stop Ruuxa from doing anything he wanted to do as long as Raina was with him.

Ruuxa and Raina Become Famous

Over the next year and a half, Ruuxa and Raina became famous. Newspapers and magazines featured stories about them. They appeared on television shows.

As the fastest land animal, adult cheetahs can run up to 70 miles per hour!

People who visited the Safari Park watched Ruuxa and Raina run on a straight track at Shiley's Cheetah Run. The track is 100 yards long, the same length as a football field. Ruuxa chased a toy zebra that was attached to a pulley. People were amazed at how fast he could run! His top speed was 70 miles per hour. Of course, Raina ran slower than Ruuxa.

Raina's top speed was 27 miles per hour.

Something's Wrong with Raina

One warm summer day when Ruuxa and Raina were two years old, the trainers noticed that Raina was limping. The veterinarians thought she might have a foot or shoulder injury, so they took X-rays.

Although the X-rays didn't show anything unusual, Raina was given some pain medicine. Raina's limp didn't go away, though, and then her shoulder began to swell.

When Raina went to the hospital for her X-rays, Ruuxa didn't like being away from her.

Aquilion
Ex: 486
Body 2.0 CE
C: CE
Se: 4/5
Im: 121/261
Ax: F1106.5
Mag: 3.8x
R

Tumor on scapula bone

Normal scapula bone

SD ZO

This is a cross-sectional view of Raina's chest.

Heart region

Lungs

The CT scan combines a series of X-ray images on a computer to create a detailed picture of the bones, blood vessels, and soft tissues in Raina's body.

Veterinarians took a closer look at Raina's shoulder by taking a CT scan of it. They were surprised by what they found: Raina had cancer. She had a big tumor in her shoulder and two smaller tumors in her body. This kind of cancer had no cure.

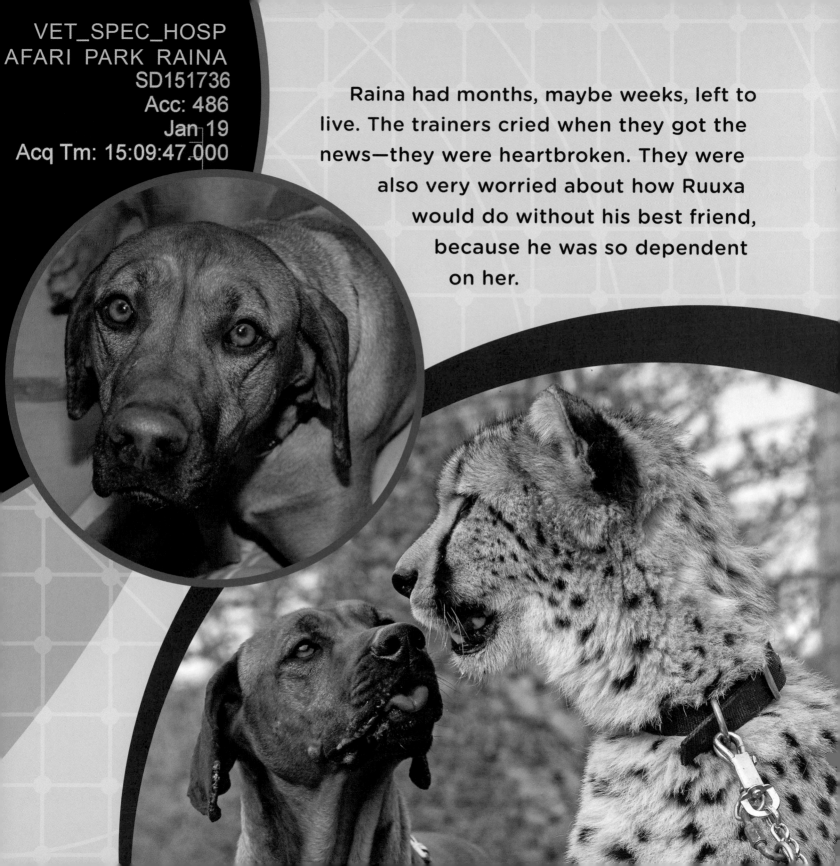

Raina had months, maybe weeks, left to live. The trainers cried when they got the news—they were heartbroken. They were also very worried about how Ruuxa would do without his best friend, because he was so dependent on her.

Here Comes Little Rae!

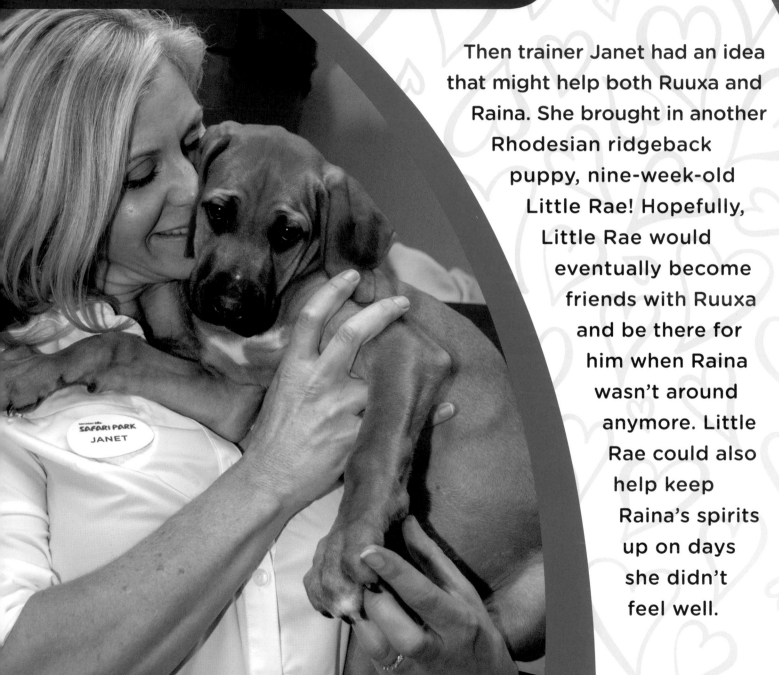

Then trainer Janet had an idea that might help both Ruuxa and Raina. She brought in another Rhodesian ridgeback puppy, nine-week-old Little Rae! Hopefully, Little Rae would eventually become friends with Ruuxa and be there for him when Raina wasn't around anymore. Little Rae could also help keep Raina's spirits up on days she didn't feel well.

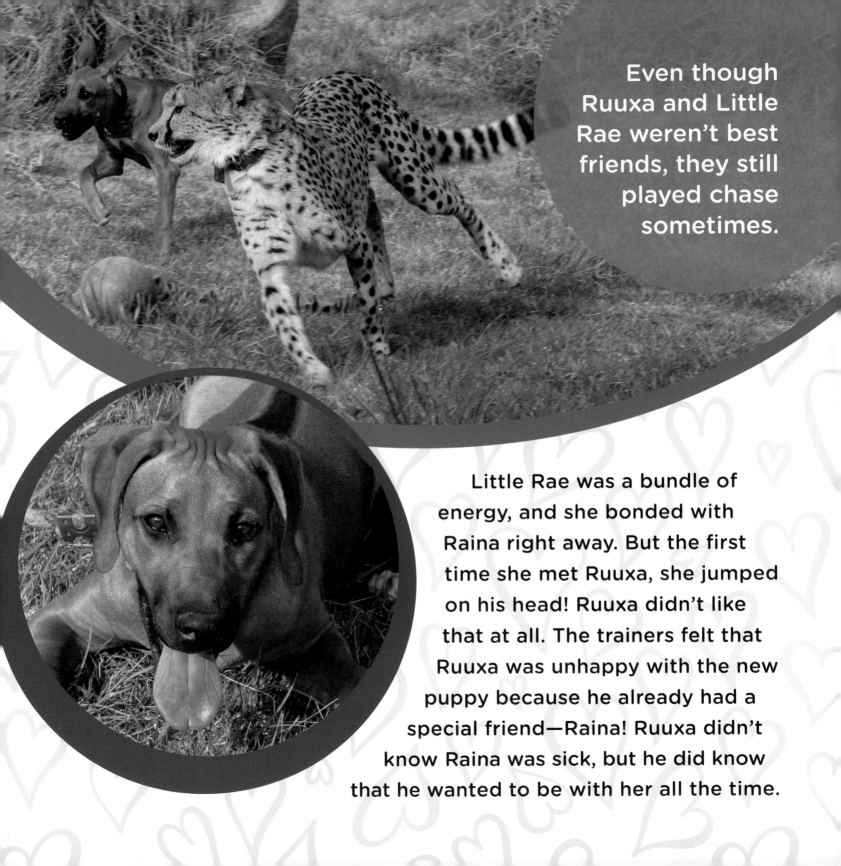

Even though Ruuxa and Little Rae weren't best friends, they still played chase sometimes.

Little Rae was a bundle of energy, and she bonded with Raina right away. But the first time she met Ruuxa, she jumped on his head! Ruuxa didn't like that at all. The trainers felt that Ruuxa was unhappy with the new puppy because he already had a special friend—Raina! Ruuxa didn't know Raina was sick, but he did know that he wanted to be with her all the time.

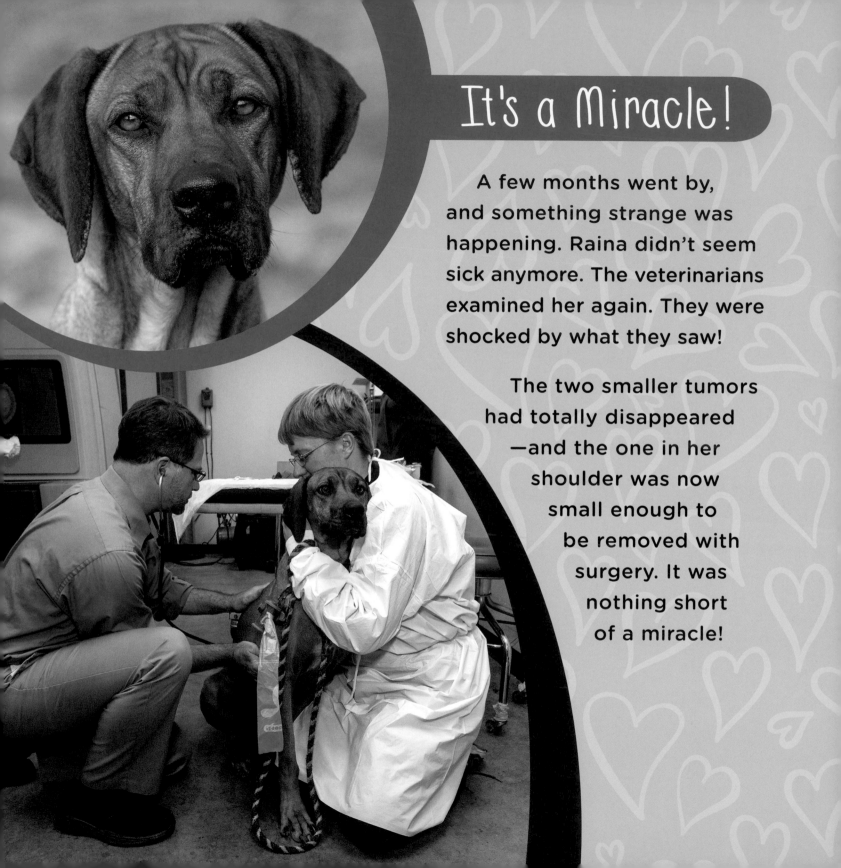

It's a Miracle!

A few months went by, and something strange was happening. Raina didn't seem sick anymore. The veterinarians examined her again. They were shocked by what they saw!

The two smaller tumors had totally disappeared —and the one in her shoulder was now small enough to be removed with surgery. It was nothing short of a miracle!

The trainers were overjoyed with the news. No one could explain what had just happened, but it didn't matter: there was a chance that Raina was going to live!

Veterinarians removed Raina's shoulder tumor. Then she started three rounds of chemotherapy, which means she was given medicine to kill any remaining cancer cells. Raina's trainer Kristyn took her to the hospital for the chemo treatments.

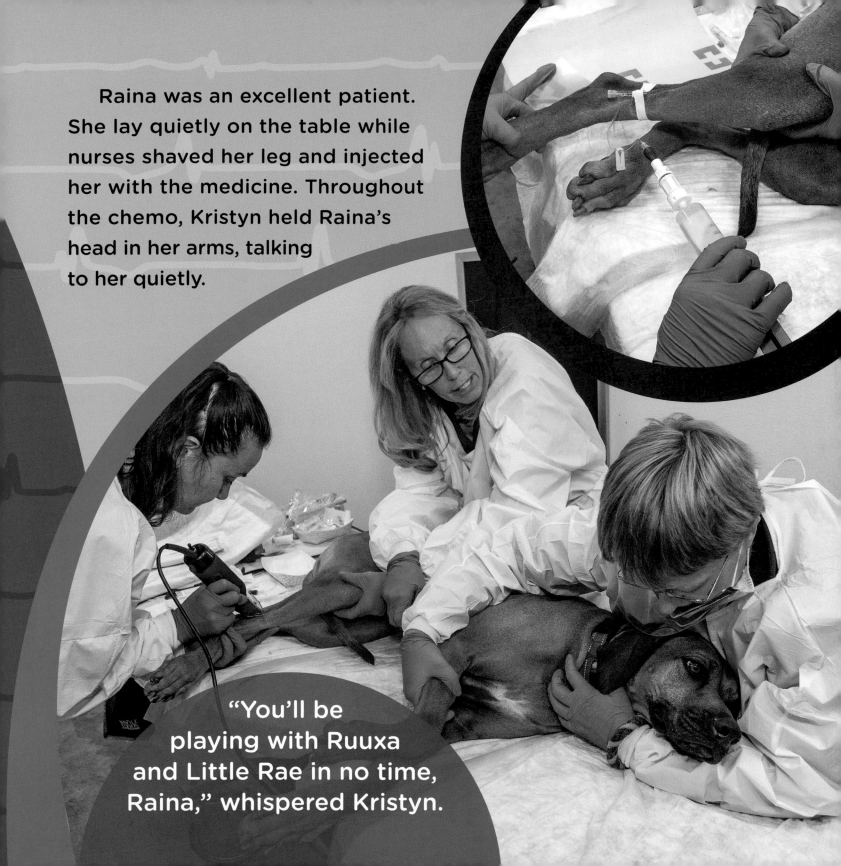

Raina was an excellent patient. She lay quietly on the table while nurses shaved her leg and injected her with the medicine. Throughout the chemo, Kristyn held Raina's head in her arms, talking to her quietly.

"You'll be playing with Ruuxa and Little Rae in no time, Raina," whispered Kristyn.

Best Friends Forever!

Today, Raina is cancer-free. She and Ruuxa spend every minute with each other, playing, going for walks, and snuggling. Little Rae joins them, too—she and Ruuxa are now friends, so the three of them live together!

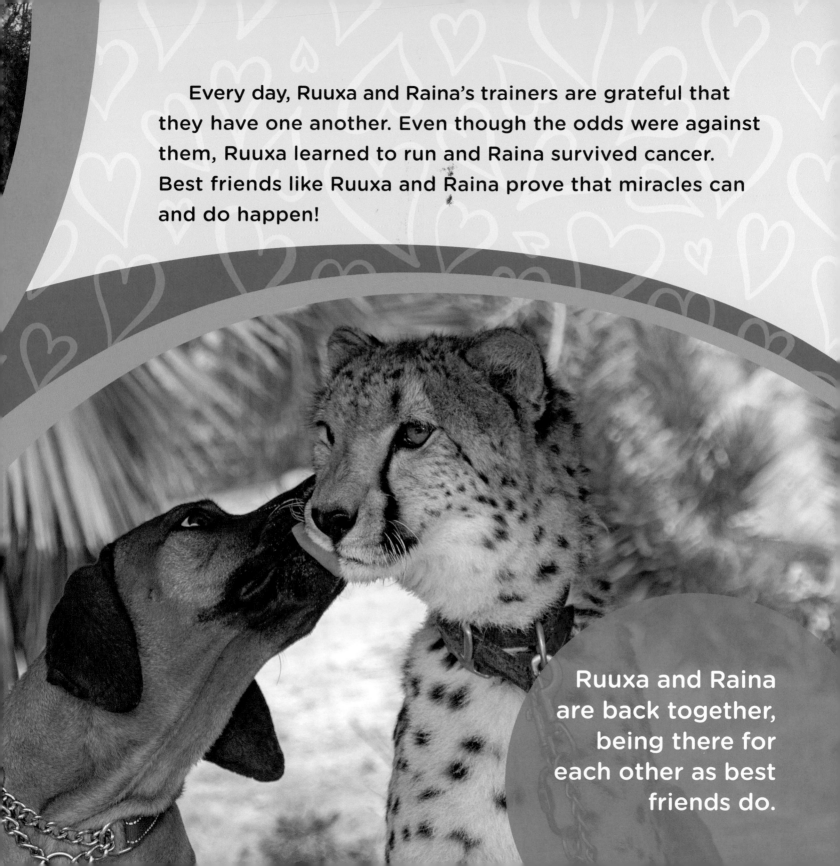

Every day, Ruuxa and Raina's trainers are grateful that they have one another. Even though the odds were against them, Ruuxa learned to run and Raina survived cancer. Best friends like Ruuxa and Raina prove that miracles can and do happen!

Ruuxa and Raina are back together, being there for each other as best friends do.

Cheetahs live in grasslands, dry forests, plains, and even deserts in Africa and Iran, which is in Asia.

Cheetahs are very vocal. They chirp, purr, growl, snarl, hiss, cough, moan, and bleat, but they cannot roar like lions or tigers do.

Fun Facts about Cheetahs

Usually, cheetah moms give birth to two to four cubs, but some litters have as many as eight cubs.

A cheetah's skin is covered with black spots, just like their fur, and the black fur grows out of those spots.

As the fastest land animal on Earth, cheetahs can run up to 70 miles per hour, but only for a short time and distance. That's the same speed as cars drive on the freeway.

Cheetahs take down their prey by hooking their legs and tripping them.

The black "tear tracks" under a cheetah's eyes help cut down the sun's glare when it is hunting.

Cheetahs are carnivores, which means they eat other animals such gazelles, impalas, wildebeests, and even zebras.

Cheetahs' claws are nonretractable and sharp like cleats, giving them great traction when they run.

Fun Facts about Rhodesian Ridgebacks

Rhodesian ridgebacks are named for the ridges that run down their spines. Some ridgebacks, like Raina, don't have ridges.

Rhodesian ridgebacks were first bred in Rhodesia (now Zimbabwe), Africa, to hunt animals like lions. They used to be called African lion hounds. Now they are mostly family pets.

Where Cheetahs Live in the World

ASIA

IRAN

AFRICA

Indian Ocean

NAMIBIA

Atlantic Ocean

**CHEETAHS ARE ENDANGERED!
THERE ARE LESS THAN 7,000 LEFT IN THE WILD.**

Threats to Cheetahs:

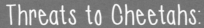

- Habitat loss
- Shortage of prey animals
- Being killed by ranchers, who think cheetahs are eating their livestock, even though other predators are usually to blame
- Illegal pet trade
- Hunting for their skin
- Tourists interfering with cheetahs that are hunting

Good News:

In Namibia, many ranchers protect their livestock by using Anatolian shepherds to chase cheetahs and other predators away. This, plus teaching the local people about the importance of wildlife, is helping Namibian cheetah populations recover.